CRAZY PATCHWORK

NORMA SLABBERT

δελος

CAPE TOWN

© 1991 Delos, 40 Heerengracht, Cape Town

Also available in Afrikaans as *Dolle Laswerk*

Translated by Wilna Swart
Photography by Anton de Beer
Styling by Norma Slabbert and Suzette Kotzé
Illustrations by Wiekie Theron
Cover design by Abie and Jasmine Fakier
Typeset in 10 on 12 pt ITC Century Light
Printed and bound by Associated Printing, Cape Town

First impression 1991

ISBN 1-86826-176-X

Contents

Introduction   4

The charm of Victorian crazy patchwork   4

Requirements   6

Choice of fabric   6

Hints on colour   7

Embroidery stitches   8

Crazy patchwork techniques   11
Basic method 1: Hand   11
Basic method 2: Sewing machine   12
Basic method 3: Iron-on interfacing   14
Basic method 4: Wadding   15

Patterns
Coat-hanger cover   17
Wine-red wall hanging   18
Christmas dress and Christmas card holder   20

Variations of crazy patchwork – a modern approach   22
Variation 1: With fusible web   22
Variation 2: Crazy patchwork derived from log cabin patchwork   25
Variation 3: Crazy patchwork derived from strip patchwork   26
Variation 4: Crazy patchwork and appliqué combined   28

Finish, hanging methods and care of crazy patchwork articles   30

Bibliography   31

Acknowledgements   32

Introduction

Crazy patchwork is once again the height of fashion. The Victorians started it and made it familiar, famous and infamous.

With the emphasis on recycling which already runs through our daily existence like a golden thread, the time is right for the revival of this kind of fabric work. Each remnant can be put to work in a useful way and experimentation is strongly emphasised.

Old fabric from used articles of clothing, ties, scarves, sheets, tablecloths and curtains are used to make new articles. Even the smallest piece of fabric, ribbon or lace can be joined to create a bigger piece of fabric with which utility articles can be made. This is economising at its best.

Contemporary crazy patchwork is easy, quick and very suitable for the quilt lover who does not have the skill, taste, time or patience that traditional patchwork requires. It can be done on the sewing machine or by hand and does not require any particular sewing skills. The charm and success lie in the choice, colour and shape of the little pieces of fabric.

This book covers the traditional Victorian approach, but also uses it as the point of departure for the development of new possibilities of this centuries-old art form.

The charm of Victorian crazy patchwork

Crazy patchwork was very popular in the late nineteenth century and the praises of this craze were sung in stories and poems, copied on fabric and greeting cards and marketed by merchants, by mail order businesses and at exhibitions.

Women's magazines praised readers for their ingenuity and creative contribution to reusing fabric and encouraged them to use all their remnants and articles of clothing. Scarves, braids, cigar labels, lace, frills, ties, gloves and usable parts of old articles of clothing were all used for crazy patchwork.

The Victorians had a preference for the exotic, extraordinary and unknown. As a result of renewed trade relations with Japan they were fascinated by the mystery of the East and Japanese designs were abundantly used in crazy patchwork. Periodicals described this craze as a "Japanese confusion".

The regularity and symmetry of the early American patchwork made way for the more exotic, irregular approach of the Japanese design. Cotton was out of fashion and quilters worked in luxury fabrics such as silk, satin, velvet and brocade. The approach was spontaneous and lacked any obvious design, therefore it was named "crazy patchwork".

Articles of crazy patchwork suited the frippery of the Victorian decor and style: the heavy fabrics, dark wood, upholstered furniture and novelties. The colours of the Victorian era — rich shades of brown, muted yellow, purple, red, wine-red, green, blue, dove-grey and rust-brown — dominated.

The crazy patchwork fad started in America and had spread to Britain by 1884. In Britain it was the height of fashion to do embroidery and this influenced crazy patchwork. Articles were sometimes used to exhibit the maker's skill with the needle and were often overdecorated. Elaborate embroidery stitches were used to create motifs of flowers, leaves, spiders, animals, butterflies, fans or lanterns. This was not always done in good taste, but in this way many new stitches were developed and survived to be used by descendants. Names, dates and verses were sometimes written on small pieces of fabric in ink, and the work became an heirloom with personal and sentimental value. Sometimes motifs were done on the fabric in oil paint, as in the traditional crazy patchwork quilt in the photograph.

Utility crazy patchwork articles had an inner layer, while exhibition articles were often not quilted and had no linings.

Victorian crazy patchwork was colourful, original and individualistic. It indicated a break with the traditional approach and is therefore an art form that is the answer to today's spontaneous approach to fabric art, the challenge of reusing old fabric and the joy of using remnants creatively.

This quilt was made in America in the late nineteenth century. In 1900 John Wittele won it in a lottery in Idaho. In 1908 he emigrated to South Africa and brought the quilt along. His daughter, Ms M.E. Solms, donated it to the South African Cultural History Museum in 1975.

Requirements

Sewing scissors

Needlework scissors
A small pair of scissors with sharp ends is ideal for cutting embroidery thread and the smallest remnant.

Pins
Long, sharp, thin pins for fine fabrics such as silk and satin are essential.

Ruler and a set square

Thimble (optional)

Quilting frame (optional)

Iron
Iron all fabric before you start cutting it. Iron every small piece of fabric after it has been sewed and folded over.

Wadding
Polyester wadding is available in various widths and is washable.

Polyester stuffing (for cushions)

Thread
Use the thread most suited to the fabric and purpose of the article. Cotton machine, embroidery and crochet thread have a mat appearance and is commonly available. Pearl cotton and string cotton thread is more glossy and is exceptionally suitable for crazy patchwork. Use a needle with a big enough eye so that the gloss of the thread is not damaged.

Needles
Use an embroidery needle suitable for the fabric and embroidery thread. A needle that is too thick will leave holes in the fabric. Sizes 3 to 10 are suitable for hand embroidery. The higher the number, the finer and shorter the needle. Crewel needles are used for thinner thread and fabric and chenille needles for thicker thread and fabric.

Fusible web with a paper base
(''Fusa Fix'' or ''Thermo Grip'')
Use fusible web to melt together the tiniest remnants to create a new length of fabric. This is used in the modern approach in particular.

Iron-on interfacing (''Staflex'')
This has a pure cotton base with a layer of glue on the upper side.

Fabric
Crazy patchwork consists of the following layers:
■ Base fabric consisting of thin calico, cotton or old linen.
■ A top layer of remnants cut into tiny pieces and sewed together as well as onto the base fabric. Traditionally velvet, satin and brocade were used, but any fabric is suitable. Experiment with remnants of silk, satin, brocade, cotton, velvet or denim and fabric of old articles of clothing, ties, gloves, small lace handkerchiefs, curtains, tablecloths and hair ribbons.
■ An interfacing to give body and to strengthen fabrics. Iron-on interfacing works well.
■ A back layer as lining of the completed patchwork article.

Choice of fabric

■ Use fabrics with different textures. This influences the visual value of the colours and makes the completed work more interesting.
■ Use combinations of printed fabrics. Alternate small designs with medium-sized and bigger patterns. Paisley or exotic batik designs give life and movement.
■ Medium-sized designs are most commonly available, but be careful of using too many of them — they can ''merge'' and create a confused impression.

■ Geometric designs such as dots, stripes and small squares give brightness and movement. Alternate the direction of the stripes by placing the pieces of fabric in various positions.
■ Use printed and plain fabrics and even the reverse side of fabrics together.
■ Buy smaller quantities, but a large variety.
■ Choose fabric suitable for the article — use washable, firm fabric for the utility articles and retain the luxury fabrics for exhibits. The different

fabrics must weigh approximately the same and have the same method of cleaning. Keep the finish in mind — the pieces of fabric must not stretch or fray, but must fold easily. Furthermore: is it shrink, stain and fadeproof? Silk, for example, is not always colourfast and can be faded and weakened by sunlight.
■ Irregularity in fabric can create an interesting effect. Do ask for discount on such fabric.

Hints on colour

■ Traditional crazy patchwork was done in rich, dark colours and a lot of black was used.

■ Do read more on the theory of colour to enable you to apply it, but when working with fabric it is good to maintain a balance between theory and instinct. The instinctive approach is choosing colours because they "feel" right. A sense of colour develops with experience.

■ Experiment with colour. Lay out the fabric and arrange it in random combinations. Determine which pieces of fabric coordinate well to create a satisfactory combination of colours.

■ Collect as many shades of one colour as possible and alternate them in the same article. A subtle diversity of colours renders the work rich and interesting.

■ Maintain a balance between light and dark, bright and dull colours.

■ Keep in mind that colours are influenced by the colours of neighbouring pieces of fabric. A piece of black fabric adjacent to a colour will illuminate it, while white will subdue it.

■ Colour is influenced by the number, size and arrangement of the pieces of fabric — therefore adapt to this as the article progresses.

■ Light influences colour. Keep in mind where the article will be used. Choose fabric in natural light, but note how electric light changes it.

■ Small designs merge when viewed from a distance, but also lend texture. They can therefore replace plain fabric.

■ Choose complementary, but not dominating colours of embroidery thread to go with the fabric. Embroidery thread in one colour binds separate units and subdues the irregular effect of crazy patchwork. Two shades of one colour of embroidery thread can often be used together in one stitch. The Victorians often used little bits of leftover thread in one article.

Embroidery stitches

Decorating with embroidery stitches is the unique characteristic of crazy patchwork. There are hundreds of embroidery stitches, but crazy patchwork requires knowledge of only a few basic stitches. In the modern approach stitches may be omitted completely.

■ Experiment with stitches. Learn to do new ones, but design your own by combining existing stitches. It does not matter if your stitches do not resemble those in the diagram. Regard it as your own, unique stitch.

■ Make a stitch cloth if you are not yet familiar with stitches.

■ Stitches have to be firm, but not so tight that they gather the fabric. First do a few stitches on a remnant to make sure of the tension.

■ Keep the work neat on the wrong side. It is better to cast off and start again than leave long loops on the wrong side. Cut off loose threads.

■ Start on the wrong side, leaving a 5 cm length of thread. Do not start with a knot when working with silk or satin.

■ Stitches must be a little bigger than required at corners and curves as these tend to shrink.

Basic stitches

Fly stitch

Bring the thread through at the top left, hold it down with the left thumb, insert the needle to the right on the same level a little distance from where the thread first emerged and make a small stitch downwards at the centre with the thread below the needle. Pull through and insert the needle again below the stitch at the centre (fig 1) and bring it through in position for the next stitch. This stitch may be worked singly, in horizontal rows (fig 1) or vertically (fig 2).

French knot

Bring the thread out at the required position, hold the thread down with the left thumb and encircle the thread twice with the needle as in fig 1. Still holding the thread firmly, twist the needle back to the starting point and insert it close to where the thread first emerged (see arrow). Pull the thread through to the back and secure for a single French knot or pass onto the position of the next stitch as in fig 2.

Cretan stitch

Bring the needle through centrally at the left-hand side, making a small stitch on the lower line, the needle pointing inwards and with the thread under the needle point, as shown in fig 1. Make a stitch on the upper line, the thread under the needle as shown in fig 2. Continue in this way until the shape is filled.

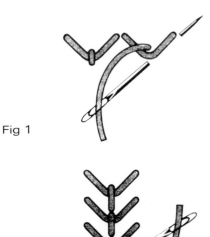

Fig 1

Fig 2

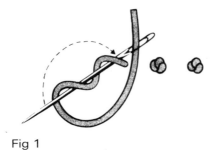

Fig 1

Fig 2

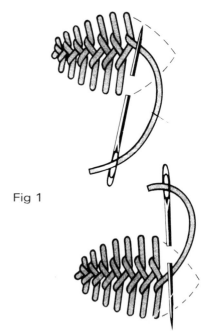

Fig 1

Fig 2

Featherstitch

Bring the needle out at the top centre, hold the thread down with the left thumb, insert the needle a little to the right on the same level and make a small stitch at the centre, keeping the thread under the needle point. Next, insert the needle a little to the left on the same level and make a stitch at the centre, keeping the thread under the needle point. Work these two movements alternately.

Buttonhole stitch

Bring the thread out on the lower line and insert the needle in position on the upper line, making a straight downward stitch with the thread under the needle point. Pull up the stitch to form a loop and repeat. Work the stitches close together.

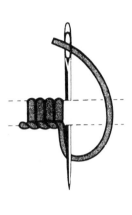

Chain stitch

Bring the thread out at the top of the line and hold it down with the left thumb. Insert the needle where it last emerged and bring the point out a short distance away. Pull the thread through, keeping the working thread under the needle point.

Herringbone stitch

Bring the needle out on the lower line at the left side and insert on the upper line a little to the right, making a small stitch to the left with the thread below the needle. Next, insert the needle on the lower line a little to the right and make a small stitch to the left with the thread below the needle. Then, insert the needle on the lower line a little to the right and make a small stitch to the left with the thread above the needle. These two movements are worked throughout. For the best effect, the fabric lifted by the needle and the spaces between the stitches should be of equal size. This stitch can be interwoven with a matching or contrasting thread. Use a round, pointed needle for weaving and do not pick up any of the fabric.

Fern stitch

This stitch consists of three straight stitches of equal length radiating from the same central point – A. Bring the thread through at A and make a straight stitch to B. Bring the thread through again at A and make another straight stitch to C. Repeat once more at D and bring the thread through at E to commence the next three radiating stitches. The central stitch follows the line of the design.

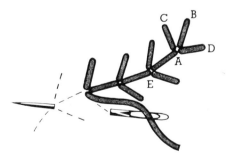

Slip stitch

Slip stitch is usually used for blind appliqué work and ought to be virtually invisible. Insert the needle vertically through the base from below, with the tip emerging against the edge of the shape, and make a small straight stitch in the fold of the hem's edge. Repeat every 5 mm.

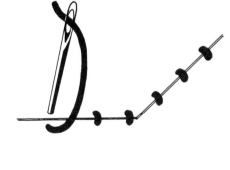

Straight stitch or single satin stitch

These are single-spaced stitches worked either in a regular or in an irregular manner. Sometimes the stitches are of varying size. The stitches should be neither too long nor too loose.

Satin stitch

Work straight stitches closely together across the shape, as shown in the diagram. If desired, running stitch or chain stitch may be worked first to form a padding underneath for a raised effect. Care must be taken to keep a good edge. Do not make the stitches too long, as they are liable to be pulled out of position.

Backstitch

Bring the thread through on the stitch line, then make a small backward stitch through the fabric. Bring the needle through again a little in front of the first stitch. Make another stitch, inserting the needle at the point where it first came through.

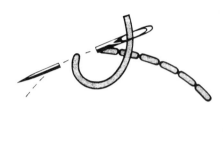

Combine these basic stitches to create your own stitches

1. Herringbone stitch and straight stitch
2. Chain stitch
3. Large fly stitch and small fly stitch
4. Straight stitch and French knots
5. Straight stitch and French knots
6. Fern stitch and satin stitch
7. Cross stitch and French knots
8. Chain stitch and straight stitch
9. Fly stitch and French knots
10. Straight stitch and French knots
11. Featherstitch, straight stitch and French knots
12. French knots and straight stitch

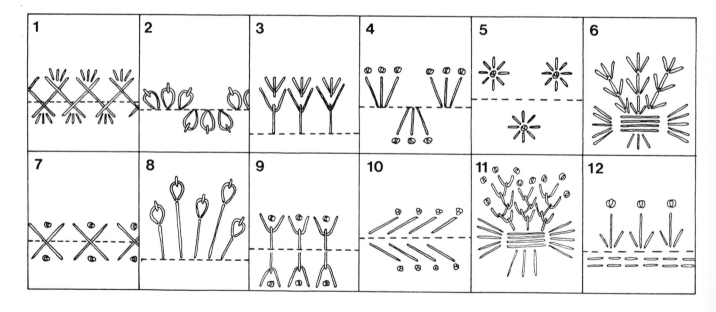

Crazy patchwork techniques

Basic method 1: Hand

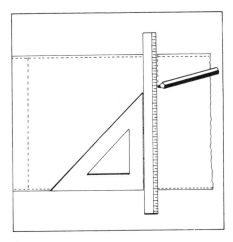

1
Use a set square and ruler and cut out a 25 × 25 cm square of cotton base fabric.

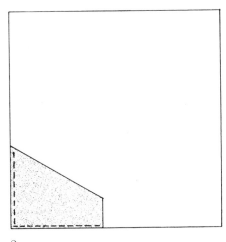

2
Cut a corner patch, place it right side up on the base fabric and tack the two outer edges.

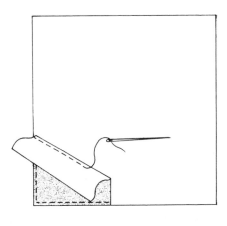

3
Place a second patch onto the corner patch with the right sides against one another. One edge of one patch must fit exactly onto that of the other patch. Sew the edges using backstitch and leaving a 5 mm seam allowance.

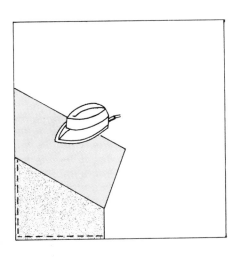

4
Fold the second patch back, right side up, and press gently.

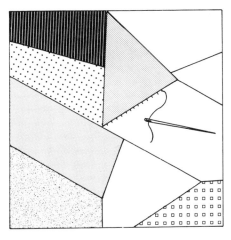

5
Sew the patches together one by one in the same way until the base fabric is covered. You will find that some seams are not sewed. Fold in the loose edges and sew them with small invisible slip stitches to the right side of the bottom patch.

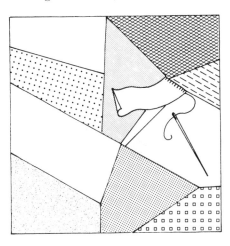

6
If parts of the base fabric protrude, sew small scraps of fabric over them. Press the edges of these **scraps** to the reverse side and sew them or using slip stitches.

11

7

Cover the joins with embroidery stitches – see photograph.

Hints

■ *Pin the patches together beforehand to get an overall impression.*
■ *The base fabric may shrink somewhat or become warped because of the embroidery stitches; therefore it is necessary to shape it with the aid of a set square and ruler after it has been decorated. When the article is made out of squares the base fabric must always be cut 1 cm bigger than the completed square is expected to be.*

Luxury fabrics consisting of velvet, silk and old ties were used for this traditional piece of work.

Basic method 2: Sewing machine

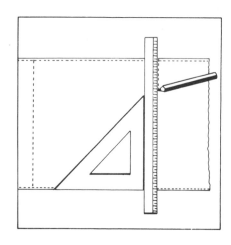

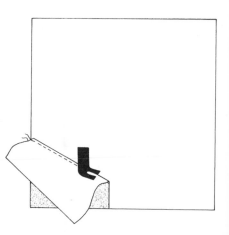

1

Use a set square and ruler and cut out a square of cotton base fabric, 25 × 25 cm.

2

Cut a corner patch, place it right side up on the base fabric and sew the outer edges together.

3

Place a second patch on the corner patch, right sides against one another. One edge of one patch must fit exactly onto that of the other patch. Sew the two patches together, allowing for a 5 mm seam.

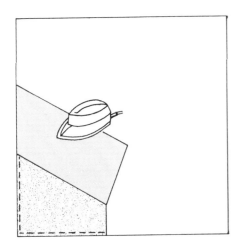

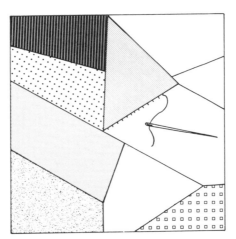

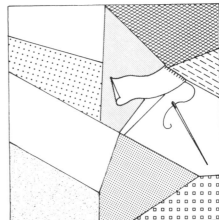

4
Fold the second patch back, right side up, and press gently.

5
Sew the patches together one by one in this way until the base fabric is covered. You will find that some seams cannot be sewed on the sewing machine, round seams in particular. Fold the loose edges in and sew to the bottom patch with small invisible slip stitches on the right side.

6
If parts of the base fabric protrude, sew small patches of fabric over them. Press the edges of these over to the wrong side and sew with slip stitches.

7
Cover the joins with decorative machine stitches or embroider by hand – see photograph. The stitches may also be omitted completely, as with the quilt on the cover.

Hint
■ *Use the machine method for everyday utility articles that will be washed often or for articles intended for the nursery that have to be wear-and-tear resistant.*

Machine stitches are used to decorate the article and to strengthen it for everyday use.

Basic method 3: Iron-on interfacing

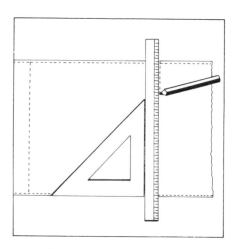

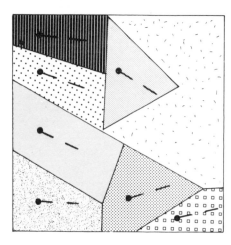

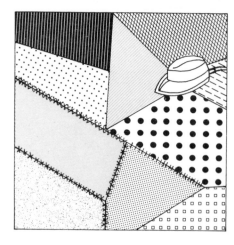

1

Use a set square and ruler and cut a square, 25 × 25 cm, of base fabric consisting of iron-on interfacing. Place it with the glossy side facing upwards.

2

Arrange the patches on the interfacing right sides up, edges overlapping slightly. Pin each piece of fabric down in the middle with one pin (more pins may stretch the fabric).

3

Press carefully and remove the pins as you progress. The fabric now adheres to the interfacing.

4

Cover the joins with embroidery stitches or decorative machine stitches — see photograph.

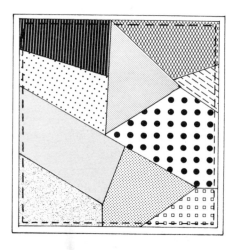

5

Strengthen the article by sewing on a back layer. Sew through all the layers.

Use small oblong or square pieces of fabric for this new, original approach. Cover the joins of the patches with machine stitches instead of hand-embroidered stitches. Interesting texture and colour effects can be created with thread.

Hint

■ *Fusible web is also suitable for this method. Place it with the paper layer facing downwards and arrange the patches right side up on top of it, edges overlapping slightly. Press gently to melt the patches together. Pull off the paper layer and place the "new" piece of fabric on a base fabric. Press again gently to melt the two pieces of fabric together. First experiment with the fabric to determine the effect – not all kinds of fabric work equally well. This is an excellent way of reusing the smallest remnants and creating a new piece of fabric. This is crazy patchwork done in the modern and most economic way.*

Basic method 4: Wadding

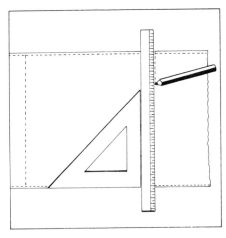

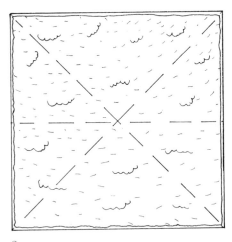

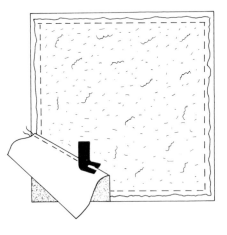

1
Use a set square and ruler and cut a square of cotton base fabric, 25 × 25 cm. Cut a piece of wadding of the same size.

2
Tack and sew the wadding to the base fabric, allowing 5 mm for a seam. The seam allowance of the wadding may be cut off if it is too thick.

3
Place the base fabric facing downwards, with the wadding facing upwards. Cut out a small corner patch, place it right side up on top of the base fabric and tack the outer edges. Place a second patch on top of the corner patch with their right sides against one another. One edge of one patch must fit exactly onto that of the other. Sew the cut-off edges together, allowing for a 5 mm seam.

Denim is ideal for this method. Use old articles of clothing and cut the little patches from different parts of the articles to get as many colour variations as possible. Make a serviceable, strong quilt for the nursery using this method and adapt the embroidery stitches to the fabric.

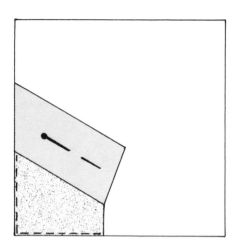 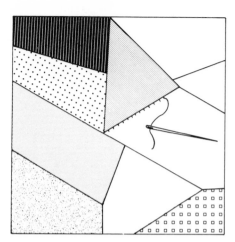 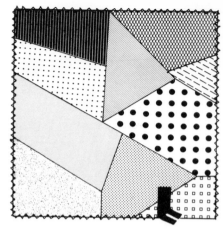

4
Fold the second patch back, right side up, and pin it down lightly.

5
Sew the patches together in the same way until the base fabric is covered. You will find that some seams cannot be stitched on the sewing machine, round seams in particular. Fold the loose edges in and sew to the bottom patch by using small invisible slip stitches on the right side.

6
Sew the edge of the completed square with ordinary or zigzag stitch. Decorate the piece with embroidery stitches if preferred.

Coat-hanger cover

Coat-hanger covers can look dirty and neglected very quickly. Use this pattern to make a practical, washable cover that is simultaneously a showpiece in your wardrobe. This is also an ideal gift for a bride.

Requirements

- 50 × 60 cm white cotton fabric
- Remnants of washable fabric in shades of white and cream
- Matching embroidery thread
- Cream crochet thread
- Cream or white lace
- Cream or white ribbon
- Wooden hanger
- Cold glue

Method

1

Place the hanger on newspaper and trace the upper edge with a pencil. Draw vertical lines of 9 cm each downwards on either side. Join the 2 ends and cut out the paper pattern.

2

Use the pattern for cutting 4 panels from the cotton fabric – a base fabric each for the front and back plus the 2 back panels. Use basic method 1 or 2 of the techniques and cover the pieces of base fabric with remnants. Decorate the 2 completed panels with embroidery stitches. Place the 4 panels on top of one another and trim to the same size. Complete the front: place the base fabric and back panel with the right sides against one another and sew the sides and the top. Turn inside out.

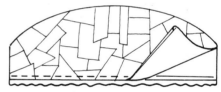

3

Fold the lower edges in and place the lace between the two layers. Sew on the right side.

4

Complete the back in the same way. Place the front and back panels right sides against one another, and sew the sides and upper part, allowing 5 mm for a seam. Leave an opening of 1 cm in the centre on top for the hanger's hook.

5

Turn the cover inside out and press gently. Decorate it with loose little bows or roses that can be removed when the cover is washed. Use crochet thread and cover the hook of the hanger with blanket stitch. Seal the ends with cold glue. Pull the cover over the hanger.

Wine-red wall hanging

Completed size: 98 × 78 cm (can be adapted as preferred)

Requirements

■ 60 × 80 cm cotton fabric for base (sheeting is ideal)
■ 200 × 28 cm black fabric for border strips
■ 200 × 40 cm wine-red fabric for border strips
■ 100 × 80 cm black fabric for back layer
■ Remnants in shades of wine-red, plum, ochre, rust and brick
■ Black embroidery thread
■ 40 × 40 cm firm cardboard

Method

1
Wash, shrink and iron the base fabric.

2
Use a set square and ruler and cut 2 pattern stencils of 19 × 19 cm and 20 × 20 cm out of the cardboard. Cut 12 squares of 20 × 20 cm, using the pattern stencil, out of the base fabric.

3
Use either basic method 1 or 2 of the techniques and cover all the squares with remnants. Make sure that a good

balance between big and small patches and an even spread of colours are maintained.

4
Press the squares gently, cut the edges even and ensure that the corners are flush by using the smaller pattern stencil. The squares are now 19 × 19 cm in size. Decorate the completed squares with embroidery stitches.

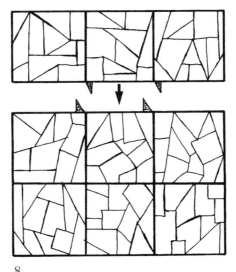

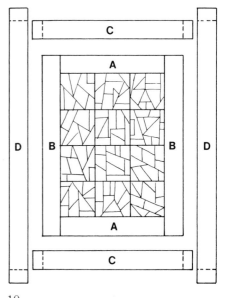

1	2	3
4	5	6
7	8	9
10	11	12

5
Place the squares in 4 rows of 3 each. Move the squares around until you have a satisfactory composition − make sure that you have an even spread of size and colour. Mark the sequences of the squares lightly on the reverse side.

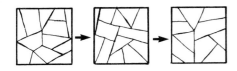

6
Join the upper 3 squares, allowing 5 mm for seams. Join the other 3 strips in the same way.

7
Press the seam allowance in different directions.

8
Pin the 4 strips to one another. Ensure that the joins are exactly opposite one another where the seams cross. Sew the strips to one another to complete the top layer. Press gently. Ensure that the seams are exactly opposite one another and that the corners are flush.

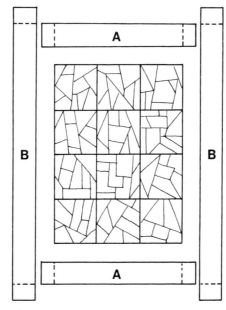

9
Cut 2 black border strips of 6 cm wide and as long as the width of the top layer plus a 5 mm seam allowance on each side − see A. Sew the 2 strips on either side of the top layer. Cut and sew another 2 black border strips for the sides of the top layer − see B.

10
Cut 2 wine-red border strips of 9 cm wide and as long as the width of the top layer and the black border strip plus a 5 mm seam allowance on either side − see C. Sew on the strips. Cut and stitch another 2 wine-red border strips for the sides of the top layer − see D. Press all the seams gently.

11
Cut a back layer of exactly the same size as the completed top layer. Tack and sew with the right sides against one another. Leave a small opening at the bottom for turning the wall hanging inside out. Turn inside out to the right side and press gently. Sew the opening with small invisible slip stitches.

12
The top layer can be tied to the back layer with black embroidery thread. Insert the needle in the corner joins from underneath and back again and then tie the 2 loose ends at the back.

Christmas dress and Christmas card holder

Christmas dress

Completed size: 84 cm in diameter (can be adapted as preferred)

Requirements

- Firm cotton for base, e.g. old sheet or tablecloth
- 85 × 85 cm fabric for back layer
- Remnants with Christmas designs and colours
- Red bias binding
- Matching thread
- Double sheet of newspaper
- Pencil
- 45 cm string
- Drawing pin

Method

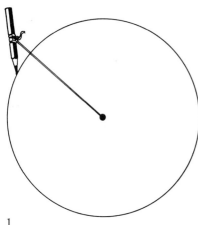

1

Tie the string around the pencil and cut off a 43 cm long piece. Fasten the other end of the string to the centre of the newspaper with a drawing pin. Pull the string taut, draw a circle and cut it out.

2

Use the paper pattern and cut a circle out of the base fabric. Fold the fabric circle into quarters and cut out a small circle with a radius of 10 cm in the centre. Cut a split running from the small circle to the outer border in a perpendicular line.

3

Use method 1 or 2 of the techniques and cover the base fabric with remnants. Decorate the completed fabric with embroidery or machine stitches (optional). Cut the edge even and sew the back layer to the base fabric. Sew the red bias binding along the border, the open split and the small circle in the centre. Press gently.

Christmas card holder

Completed size: 90 × 70 cm (can be adapted as preferred)

Requirements

- 61 × 43 cm firm white fabric for base
- 3 strips of 43 × 13 cm same fabric for pieces of base fabric for pockets
- 2 strips of 43 × 11 cm green fabric for inner horizontal border strips
- 2 strips of 80 × 11 cm same fabric for inner vertical border strips
- 2 strips of 92 × 7 cm red dotted fabric for outer horizontal border strips
- 2 strips of 61 × 7 cm same fabric for outer vertical border strips
- 92 × 72 cm fabric for back layer
- Remnants with Christmas designs and colours
- Red cotton bias binding
- Red rickrack

Method

1

Use method 1 or 2 of the techniques and cover the pieces of base fabric for the pockets with the remnants. Finish the top sides with red bias binding. Decorate the completed strips with embroidery or machine stitches (optional). Press gently.

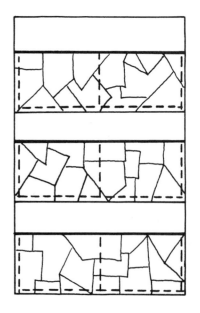

2

Space the strips and sew to the base fabric, but do not fold down the seams. Stitch a seam down the middle of each cross-strip to form a pocket.

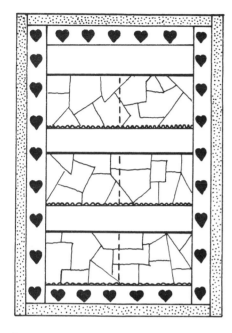

3

Stitch red rickrack over the bottom seams. Sew on the border strips. Cut little heart shapes out of the remnants and appliqué them onto the green border strips. They can also be ironed on using fusible web.

4

Place the top layer and back layer right sides against one another and sew, leaving a small opening for turning inside out. Turn inside out and press gently. Sew the opening with small invisible slip stitches. Hang according to one of the methods on p. 30.

Variations of crazy patchwork – a modern approach

Crazy patchwork is one of the most charming forms of fabric art because it offers so many possibilities. The modern point of departure is to use the basic crazy patchwork techniques to create a new piece of fabric from which utility articles can be made. With aids such as the sewing machine, fusible web and wadding it is no longer necessary to imitate the Victorians' traditional method rigidly. Use the aspects of crazy patchwork that you like, combine them with your own ideas and develop a unique style.

Variation 1: With fusible web

Wall hanging for a reading corner

Create a gay reading corner in the nursery with this wall hanging. Use the diagram on p. 24 or even use your child's artwork as inspiration for a wall hanging with a more personal touch. The fusible web technique used here is the modern way of doing crazy patchwork. In this way one can create a new piece of fabric much faster than by using the traditional method.

Requirements

- 130 × 130 cm firm black fabric for base
- 110 × 110 cm black fabric for back layer
- 4 strips of 110 × 5 cm purple fabric for border strips
- Cotton remnants in shades of green, purple, pink, orange, blue and yellow
- 1 m fusible web
- Matching thread

Method

1
Enlarge the design according to the diagram and make paper patterns of the figures.

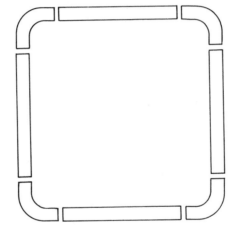

2
Cut 4 strips of 75 × 3 cm and 4 rounded corners of 3 cm in width out of the fusible web. Cut small strips out of the remnants to fill the strips of fusible web. Place the strips of fusible web on an ironing board with the paper layer facing downwards. Arrange the strips of remnants on top and melt them together with a hot iron.

3
Place the rest of the fusible web on an ironing board with the paper layer facing downwards. Place the remnants against one another on the fusible web the way you would build a puzzle. Melt them together with a hot iron. This forms the new piece of fabric out of which the motifs are cut.

4
Place the base fabric on an ironing board and arrange the 4 strips approximately 12 cm from the edges to form a frame. Place the corners so that they form a unit with the strips. Pull off the paper layer carefully and melt the strips to the base fabric with a hot iron.

5
Cut the motifs out of the new piece of fabric and carefully pull off the paper layer. Arrange the motifs on the base fabric within the frame until you are satisfied with the layout. Melt the motifs to the base fabric with a hot iron.

6
Machine-stitch detail such as trees, flowers, doors and windows. If you are anxious that they may fray or be damaged, the motifs can be strengthened with embroidery or machine stitches.

7
Place the border strips on the base fabric with the right sides against one another and sew. Place the base fabric and the back layer with the right sides against one another and sew. Leave a small opening for turning inside out. Turn the hanging inside out and sew the opening with small invisible slip stitches. Hang the hanging according to one of the methods on p. 30.

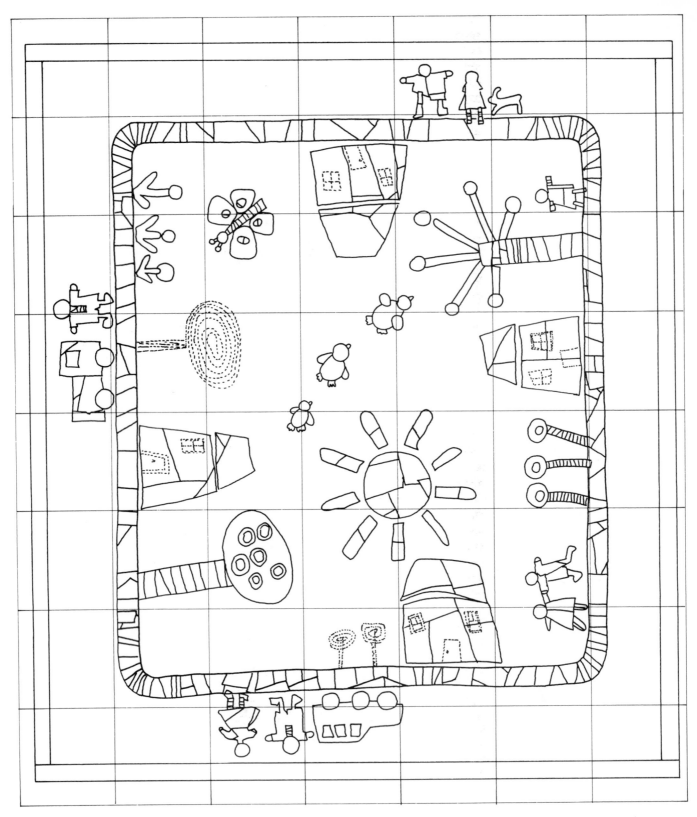

1 block = 150 mm

Variation 2: Crazy patchwork derived from log cabin patchwork

Log cabin cushion

Method

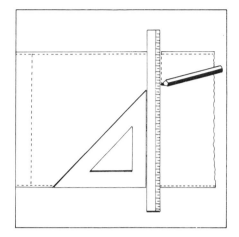

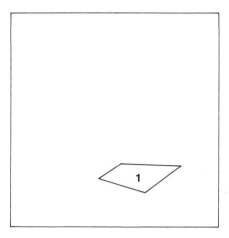

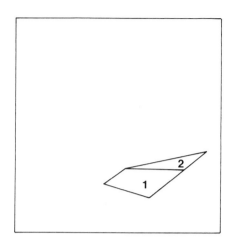

1

Use a set square and ruler and cut a square of cotton base fabric the size wanted for the cushion.

2

Cut a small piece of fabric of any shape and place it anywhere on the base fabric, except in the centre. Pin lightly with a pin.

3

Cut a number of pieces of fabric in strips of any shape. Place a second piece of fabric on the first, right sides against one another. One edge of one must fit exactly onto that of the other. Sew, leaving a 5 mm seam allowance. Fold the second piece of fabric back, right side up, and press gently.

4

Sew the pieces of fabric in a spiral around the first one by one until the base fabric is covered. You will find that the strips become longer as you progress and a particular colour or design may dominate. Prevent this by joining 2 different strips before placing it on the base fabric – see no. 6 in the diagram.

Variation 3: Crazy patchwork derived from strip patchwork

Strip patchwork is ideal for using long, narrow strips of remnants, e.g. strips cut from hems. The strips are usually not symmetrical and are joined randomly, the end result closely resembling crazy patchwork. The work is sewed on the sewing machine and not decorated with stitches. This method is used to make the quilt's border. The figures are made according to the fusible web technique (variation 1).

Crazy dots and stripes for the nursery

Method

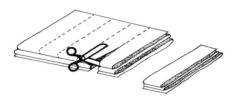

1
Fold a piece of fabric as indicated in the diagram. Old as well as new fabric can be used. Use a soft-leaded pencil and a ruler to mark strips of the same size. Cut the strips in the required lengths – cut through all the layers.

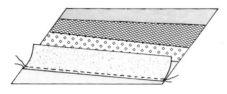

2
Arrange the strips of fabric in random colours, textures and designs until a satisfactory overall impression is achieved, and sew.

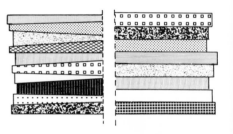

3
It can be sewed on the straight or on the bias. Alternating colour, design and width creates a more interesting effect – compare the 2 sketches.

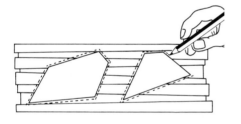

4
Use the newly created piece of fabric and cut out interesting panels that can in turn be joined.

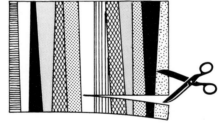

5
The new piece of fabric can also be used to make joining strips and borders. Mark and cut these in the required length and width.

6
Use the strips as ordinary fabric for borders.

Variation 4: Crazy patchwork and appliqué combined

Guinea-fowl tea cosy

Completed size: approximately 35 × 30 cm

Requirements

- 80 × 60 cm white cotton fabric for base
- Remnants in shades of red, orange, pink, purple and yellow
- Matching thread
- Fusible web

Method

1
Enlarge the diagram and cut out a paper pattern. Cut out the eye, beak and comb as separate patterns. Use the pattern and cut 4 panels out of the base fabric and 2 panels out of the fusible web.

2
Place 1 fusible web panel on an ironing board with the paper layer facing downwards and melt a fabric panel onto it. Pull off the paper layer and put the remnants on the side where the paper was, edges overlapping slightly. Press gently with a hot iron to melt the pieces of fabric to one another.

3
Use the patterns and cut 2 eyes, combs and beaks out of the remnants. Place the eyes, combs and beaks in position and melt down onto the fusible web. Complete the second panel similarly.

4
Appliqué the new panels in a new and original way by stitching rows across the whole surface. For more texture use thread in various colours. Leave 1 cm lengths of thread on the top and bottom. The frayed edges and loose pieces of thread lend an interesting effect.

5
Sew the other 2 fabric panels to the back of each appliquéd panel. This is the tea cosy's lining. Place the completed panels wrong sides against one another and sew. If an article with a more finished appearance is required, round off with bias binding.

1 block = 32 mm

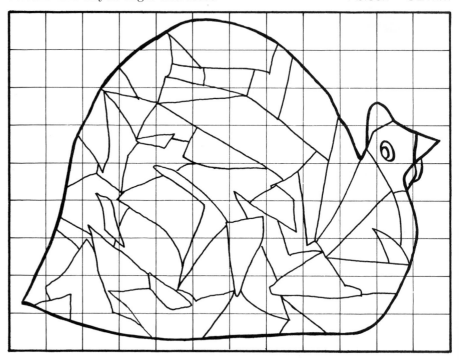

Finish, hanging methods and care of crazy patchwork articles

Finish

"Sign" your handiwork by sewing a scrap of fabric with your name, surname and address and the date embroidered on it to the wrong side of your work. The work may become an heirloom or land in a museum, and then people will know where, when and by whom it was made.

Hanging methods

A quilt can be hung in the following ways for exhibition purposes. Choose a method suitable to the article so that its weight is evenly distributed.

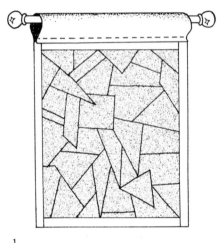

1
Sew a slide to the top edge and push a brass or wooden rod through.

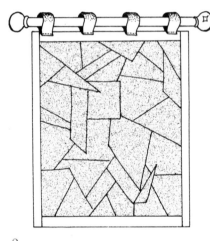

2
Sew loops to the top and push a rod through.

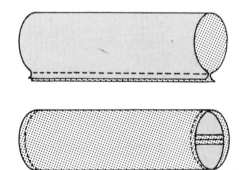

3
Make a fabric tube through which to push a rod.

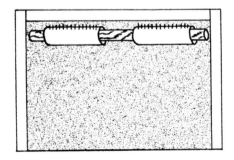

3a
Sew the tube to the back of the wall hanging. Use one tube for smaller wall hangings and two or three for bigger ones.

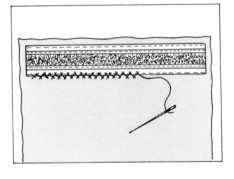

4
Sew a strip of Velcro (the fluffy part) to the back of the wall hanging, using herringbone stitch.

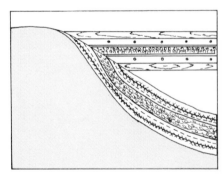

4a
Staple or glue the stiff part to a batten that can be attached to the wall with nails or screws.

Care

■ Crazy patchwork articles must preferably be stored in a cool, dry place.

■ Dust is harmful to crazy patchwork articles. Remove it as follows: tie a piece of cheesecloth to the muzzle of a vacuum cleaner. Put the article down flat, keep the muzzle just above it and vacuum the front as well as the back.

■ Light is harmful to any fabric, but especially to delicate fabric such as silk. Therefore hang the article so that it does not get direct sun or electric light.

■ If you want to put a quilt away, you can fold it, but remove it at least once every three months and fold it differently. Do not store a quilt in a plastic bag – rather fold it in an old sheet.

■ It is preferable to lay a quilt down flat on an unused bed, but you can also roll it up or hang it.

■ You can also use a quilt frame.

Bibliography

Betterton, Sheila. *Quilts and Coverlets from the American Museum in Britain.* The American Museum in Britain, Bath.
Conroy, Mary. *The Complete Book of Crazy Patchwork.* Sterling Publishing Co., New York, 1985.
Eaton, Jan. *The Complete South African Stitch Encyclopedia.* Delos, Cape Town, 1989.
Haywood, Dixie. *The Contemporary Crazy Quilt Project Book.* Crown Publishers, New York, 1977.
McMorris, Penny. *The Great American Quilt Classics: Crazy Quilts.* Quilter's Newsletter Magazine, September 1984.
Slabbert, Norma. *Patch Pictures.* Struik, Cape Town, 1988.
50 Free Style Embroidery Stitches. Delos, Cape Town, 1989.

Acknowledgements

Special thanks to:

Oubie, for my long leave
Yvette, who can now do needlework
Maurie, who was not there
Jeannie Walker, who taught me about stitches
Suzette Kotzé
South African Cultural History Museum, Cape Town
Block & Chisel Interiors, Wynberg, Cape Town

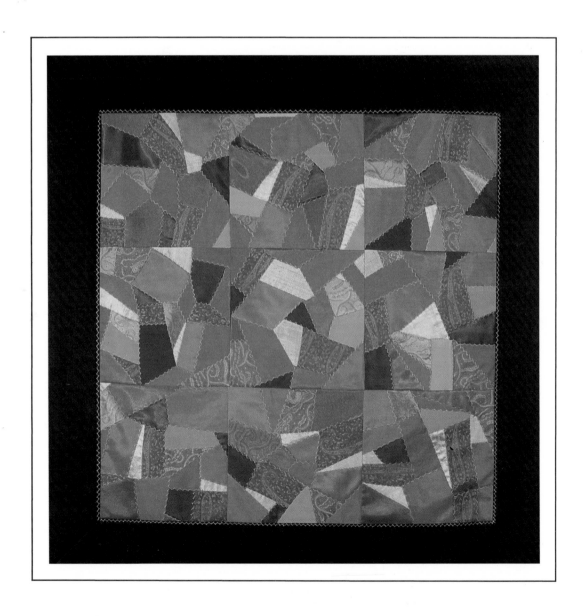